KITTENS

ELLA EARLE

summersdale

KITTENS

Summersdale Publishers Ltd
46 West Street
Chichester
West Sussex
PO19 1RP
UK

www.summersdale.com

Printed and bound in China

ISBN: 978-1-84953-547-2

Substantial discounts on bulk quantities of Summersdale books are available to corporations, professional associations and other organisations. For details contact Nicky Douglas by telephone: +44 (0) 1243 756902, fax: +44 (0) 1243 786300 or email: nicky@summersdale.com.

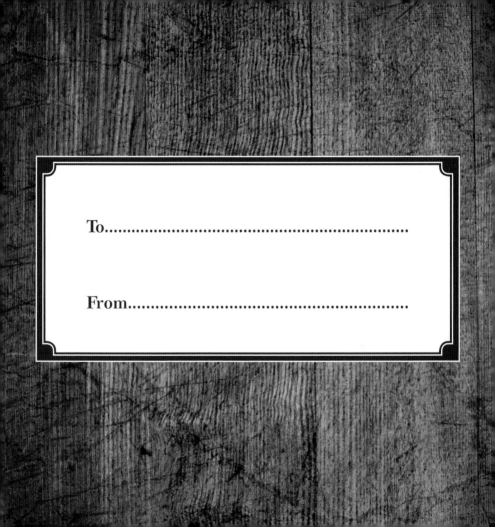

To..

From...

Introduction

Cats bring joy to our lives with their grace and elegance. But when they are kittens, we see another side to their character: they delight us with their playful frolics, their tumbling and springing, and the adorable way they snuggle and snooze. This book celebrates kittens of every variety, as they explore their new worlds and discover endless new ways to have fun!

It is impossible to keep a straight face in the presence of one or more kittens.

Cynthia E. Varnado

There are few things in life more heart-warming than to be welcomed by a cat.

Tay Hohoff

The smallest feline is a masterpiece.

Leonardo da Vinci

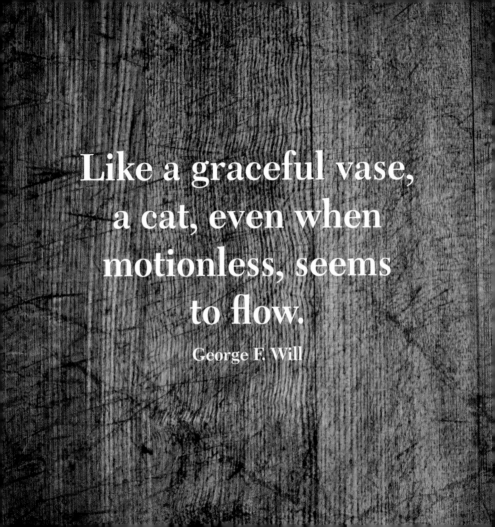

Like a graceful vase,
a cat, even when
motionless, seems
to flow.

George F. Will

A kitten is in the animal world what a rosebud is in the garden.

Robert Southey

Kittens are angels with whiskers.

Anonymous

No matter how much
cats fight, there always
seems to be plenty
of kittens.

Abraham Lincoln

I have studied many philosophers and many cats. The wisdom of cats is infinitely superior.

Hippolyte Taine

Cats are intended to teach us that not everything in nature has a purpose.

Garrison Keillor

A meow massages
the heart.

Stuart McMillan

An ordinary kitten will ask more questions than any five-year-old.

Carl Van Vechten

It is a happy talent to know how to play.

Ralph Waldo Emerson

If you can find a
path with no obstacles,
it probably doesn't
lead anywhere.

Frank Clark

Which is more beautiful – feline movement or feline stillness?

Elizabeth Hamilton

A cat's eyes are windows enabling us to see into another world.

Irish proverb

Kittens believe that all nature is occupied with their diversion.

François-Augustin de Paradis de Moncrif

If you obey all the rules,
you miss all the fun.

Katharine Hepburn

When I play with my cat, who knows if I am not a pastime to her more than she is to me?

Michel de Montaigne

A catless writer is almost inconceivable.

Barbara Holland

A cat, I am sure, could walk on a cloud without coming through.

Jules Verne

They say the test
of literary power is
whether a man can
write an inscription.
I say, 'Can he name
a kitten?'

Samuel Butler

When you invite a
kitten into your home,
you bring indoors
something slightly wild,
often unpredictable and
always entertaining.

Barbara L. Diamond

A cat is a puzzle
for which there is
no solution.

Hazel Nicholson

A kitten is chiefly remarkable for rushing about like mad at nothing whatever, and generally stopping before it gets there.

Agnes Repplier

Attitude is a little thing that makes a big difference.

Winston Churchill

What greater gift than the love of a cat?

Charles Dickens

A mother's arms are made of tenderness and children sleep soundly in them.

Victor Hugo

Curiosity is one of the great secrets of happiness.

Bryant H. McGill

A thing of beauty, strength and grace lies behind that whiskered face.

Anonymous

A kitten is the delight of a household; all day long a comedy is played out by an incomparable actor.

Champfleury

Alone we can do so little; together we can do so much.

Helen Keller

I have just been given a very engaging Persian kitten... and his opinion is that I have just been given to him.

Evelyn Underhill

There's no need for a piece of sculpture in a home that has a cat.

Wesley Bates

Friendship is a single soul dwelling in two bodies.

Aristotle

One small cat
changes coming home
to an empty house to
coming home.

Pam Brown

Forbidden things have a secret charm.

Publius Cornelius Tacitus

One of the most beautiful qualities of true friendship is to understand and to be understood.

Seneca the Younger

Life is something to do when you can't get to sleep.

Fran Lebowitz

Cats' whiskers are so sensitive, they can find their way through the narrowest crack in a broken heart.

Anonymous

The playful kitten...
is infinitely more
amusing than half the
people one is obliged to
live with in the world.

Sydney, Lady Morgan

There is nothing on this earth more to be prized than true friendship.

Thomas Aquinas

What would life be if we had no courage to attempt anything?

Vincent van Gogh

Since each of us is blessed with only one life, why not live it with a cat?

Robert Stearns

A well-spent day brings happy sleep.

Leonardo da Vinci

Kittens can happen to anyone.

Paul Gallico

If you're interested in finding out more about our books,
find us on Facebook at **Summersdale Publishers** and
follow us on Twitter at **@Summersdale**.

www.summersdale.com